THE WAY FORWARD

Leacy

BookLeaf Publishing

India | USA | UK

Presentation by BookLeaf Publishing

Web: www.bookleafpub.com

E-mail: info@bookleafpub.com

ISBN: 9789358360547

First edition 2021

INTRODUCTION

The Way Forward- a journey from the broken into the light is a compilation of poetry that will take you on a journey through some of my life's darkest pauses, to the unveiling of brighter days. As your fingers trace the pages, wherever you find me; This is how it felt from my perspective. My words, my battles, my overcoming and my victories.

As a writer I can only hope that as you feel your way through my world, you find soothing comfort in the depths of grief, heartache and hopefulness that align with your own experiences.

Throwing a wish into a wishing well creates a ripple of hope and that is all that I long to achieve. May the seeds planted within these pages, plant trees of self-belief and love that will last a lifetime. May the hurt that lies beneath some of the lines be followed by the knowing that even in the dark of night the sun will still come to rise again.

I am living proof.

DEDICATION

Raggy, my ever-constant belief system. The one who believed in me on the days I did not even believe in myself. Who met me right where I was and loved me just as I am- Here it is- this one's for us. Every real, raw, undiscovered and uncovered part of my heart. Unapologetically yours, in print. How I wish you were here to turn the pages yourself.

Em,

For your consistency, your encouragement and your ever-present guiding light. You quite literally led me to a brand-new life and for that I am eternally grateful. There are people in life that bring out the absolute best in you and you sweetheart, are absolutely that for me. I adore you.

You- The reader

I dedicate this book to you. It was written for you. May it meet you where you need it too and between the pages may you always find the seed of hope that was planted to always give a flicker of hope to light your way in life.

You were born with a purpose.

Now is the time to rise.

All in the name of his glory.

A heaven-sent enterprise,

Created by a creator to create,

Now is the time;

Sweet child.

There are moments in life that change you.

Whether or not you are prepared for it.

All of them, big and small, have the power to.

Life will meet you, head on right where you stand.

Whether you are ready or not, always expect the unexpected.

Because even in pieces,

you can still be broken-

again.

I always held us up there, with fairy-tales and romance.

However, this last dance, I feel like our hearts untied.

Whatever part of me that was bound by you-

I was finally freed of the shackles that came,

from loving you.

The road was winding,

The mood was low.

Everything was a little mellow.

The birds, the bees,

the flowers and trees too.

You came home with us today.

Just not the same way that you

used to.

-it's lonely without you

It didn't take a lot to shift her thinking.

She knew reason would seek her out, in the comfort of her own soul; but she had to be beaten, hard against the wall- to rise after a fall.

I imagine what had happened, is she lost herself in a hurricane of heartache. Of love lost and long since passed; and in doing so dismantled her own vessel from the sensation of feeling without any intention.

 She had chosen to make a definitively adamant decision to black out emotion and not feel a thing; to ultimately let the ache subside, to a numb monstrosity of emotion that just builds with the tears, suppressed deep down inside.

But like a waterfall that dries its stores in summer, her winter had seemed infinitely long, and the outpouring of her feelings were going to cascade from down in the depths of her core, watering her spring beauty, encouraging herself simply to blossom into life.

It's time, little flower, it's time

The world's going to fall apart sometimes,

and you're not going to like it.

We're all going to lose sometimes,

No matter how hard it is, you fight for it.

You're going to bleed out long after your wounds are done healing.
That will take as long as it needs to take.

But listen, can you hear me...

Do you hear those breaths passing away?

You're still here in this world,

and your heart is still beating,

The sands of time haven't run out on you

Your purpose still lives, while you do.

Your hearts still beat, beat, beating.

And your voice is still speak, speak, speaking.

They tell me there is a reason that we are all here. There's nothing to fear.

That mountain that you're climbing,

It's all about timing,

Take whatever pace you need,

So long as you breathe.

You've got to reach for that purpose,

Create from your soul,

Be who you're born to be and

Leave a sweet legacy,

Long after, long after- you are gone.

Eternally,

Your show will go on.

I have the eyes of a dreamer

& the soul of a poet.

From my primary vessel,

ink runs through my veins.

A blank canvass bathed in faith,

What masterpiece am I destined

To create?

Put the power in this pen,

Show me the lines, to weave into minds,

to show the world just how in love with you -I am.

My dear friend.

Inside of you;

You hold everything you need.

The spirit burning like a graceful beacon.

Be the lighthouse, be the light-

that guides other's home

How do you reach out to a world

that's not really listening.

How do you demand that your song be heard?

Preach it. Speak it, Breathe Love in hardened hearts, to the people
in the places that need it most.

Or wherever you feel, words of encouragement,

would most beneficially be heard.

Write it in chalk on a sidewalk,

Graffiti love upon a fence,

Make a meal for a loved one,

Give until you've nothing left.

Because someone else always needs

a little more than you do

Live a given life,

It'll only come back to you

10-fold, the dreams already sold,

The world's a better place,

Because he gave YOU,

the power to move,

And soulfully so are you.

There's so much happening, so many emotions right now; life feels like such a roller-coaster. You're already there. You just don't see it, because in the chaos that your heart's still residing in, you don't give yourself credit for how far you've already come. You're doing amazing and although at times you may feel invincible, you are seen, and you are noticed but above all else you're admired. In every shattered piece you dwell in, your shell is still whole, your heart is still yours and you're set to shine like the almighty person you were born to be. I am here for you every step of the way, encouraging and uplifting you.

I am on your side.

My heart with you was always safe,

In all my life you'd never let me down.

And with one message you were more fearful of it,

Than you were faithful to it,

But in a sense, I thank the heavens that you bailed.

Because in the brokenness of journey's planned,

I've found this most calming sense of bravery.

Like walking around in pieces,

 so carefully not to fall out of place,

but I walk anyway.

Because in my brokenness,

I am centred by faith.

With failed expectations from the imagination,

future hopes and dreams were instantly dashed,

I believe that the divine revelation right now is that life is pursuing a more powerful purpose, in this orbit of the unknown. I have faith that this intermission is just that- an intermission.

I forgive you for destroying that untarnished armour around my heart that you have solely, so carefully taken care of. I believe individually and apart our souls are somehow united together.

Wherever we reunite, I'll still meet you there.

For my soul loves you,

so well.

Stop right there,

Where you are standing.

Where you are right now.

You're stepping forward,

You honestly are-but not right now.

Not in this instance.

Pause a moment.

Take it all in.

Breathe,

then begin..

Sometimes the poetry of life is painful.

The beauty lies in the value of the lesson, no matter the brutality
we lay witness too. Sometimes we just must take those lessons and
turn those lessons into blessings.

We are all woven like tapestry, a map of all the places we've been, to
be the person we're destined to become, no matter the season, don't
give up.

You have faith. Faith is enough

She had always run from fear because as much as the idea of a little danger excited her;

One's own abilities and the rush of destiny manoeuvring through her veins terrified her. However, from this day forward she swore to herself that she would become a dream chaser. Devoting her heart and soul to upholding the talent she was blessed with. She vowed to turn love into poetry and to succumb to the desirable need to become, instinctively, the poet, when emotion takes reign. She promised herself to tell tales of life's wonderous creatures. She was devoted to the dream, of bringing the destiny she had always feared was bigger than herself-to life.

It's hard you know, hard to aim to love yourself, beyond any valid recognition, ever sought before.

When every person who's ever loved you half-heartedly, insists on scribing marks across your heart as if to obtain your attention, to falsely believe this is how it's meant to be.

That you in fact are deemed worthy of a love that fills you with self-doubt and loathing.

That your heart no matter how giving will always come up a little short, being never enough and you rushing yourself crazy-just trying to be, who they want you to be; never stopping to think, that even though you think your missions almost completed-the list of wants and desires- their ideals of how they want you to be- will never cease to end.

You can pretend that it does not harm you, that a glass that sits only ever half empty in your heart won't dry out, like the middle of the Australian dessert after a scorching hot summer-if you don't replenish your own worth and thirst; inside you will never be, a waterfall of abundance if someone else is always hydrating your validation in life. Seek to quench your own thirst, a narcissist,

will only ever leave your mouth dry.

Now she flies with the butterflies

and shines amongst the brightest of stars.

She stands in the glory of the creator,

Who is alive inside her heart.

I love morning light, the way it shines so gloriously, that it would be unforgiving to not simply bask in its splendour, even just for a moment.

To simply breathe in and be perfectly aware of its presence; partnered exquisitely with fresh coffee, enticing its way up from my lap.

Seducing my senses with its existence.

In those moments, the first of the morning

When my hair is a mess and my body is still on the journey to awake-it's right there in that shimmering light, where you simply know,

If only for this moment right here, today is a new day and right now, all is so blissfully right with the world

Whoever it is that you are,

Is enough; all that you have to offer the world,

is your wonderful, magnificent, authentic self.

Show up and serve it in all your glory

They say wisdom comes with age, but I have always had the ever-present feeling,

that I was wise beyond my years. I've always felt things on an empathetic level,

whether others were aware of that or not.

My soul has always felt so familiar, as though I've lived this journey for a thousand years and only now in this shell, I've felt at home.

As eternal as my inner being undoubtedly feels, I still find a whimsical notion in my momentary presence.

After all these years on earth there are days where I still have no clue- and that, is exhilarating; Because as much as not having it all figured out scares the life out of me, I know that the guides inside this heart and soul of mine, are still feeling their way; and when they feel, they move-

my god do I know,

without hesitation and undeniable synchronicity,

 I am undoubtedly aware in those very moments-that I am in fact-purposefully alive.